Wonders of Rivers

Written by Rae Bains

Illustrated by Yoshi Miyake

Troll Associates

Library of Congress Cataloging in Publication Data

Bains, Rae.
   Wonders of rivers.

   Summary: Briefly discusses the characteristics,
origins, formation, and uses of rivers.
   1. Rivers—Juvenile literature.   [1. Rivers]
I. Miyake, Yoshi.   II. Title.
GB1203.8.B34   551.48'3   81-7423
ISBN 0-89375-570-2   AACR2
ISBN 0-89375-571-0 (pbk.)

Just about anywhere you live, there is a river near you. Rivers flow past small towns and big cities. Rivers run down mountains. Rivers flow to the ocean. Rivers run through forests. Even in the desert, there are rivers.

Some rivers are very short. Others are thousands of miles long. The longest river in the United States is the Mississippi. It is almost 2,350 miles, or 3,760 kilometers, long!

Rivers can be almost straight as an arrow. Or they can curve like a snake twisting through the grass.

Some rivers are very narrow. Others are so wide that a person standing on one side cannot see someone standing on the other side. The Amazon River, in South America, is 90 miles, or 144 kilometers, wide in some places.

There are rivers that begin as tiny trickles of water from a lake. Other rivers begin as water bubbling up from under the ground. Most rivers start as rain or snow that falls on mountains and hills.

Winter snow covers the tops of mountains. In spring, the snow melts slowly. It starts to trickle down the mountainside. It forms tiny streams.

Soon, many tiny streams join together to make bigger streams. They run down the sides of the mountain. The tiny streams are like the smallest branches of a tree. Where they join together, they are like the big branches of a tree. And where all the streams run together, it is like the trunk of a tree. This is the river.

Spring storms add rain to the streams of melted snow. The streams bubble as they swirl down the mountainside and tumble over the edges of large rocks.

The fast-flowing river breaks little pieces off the rocks in its path. The water pushes hard against the soil on both sides of the river, loosening sand and stones and plants. Rock, sand, and plants—everything that falls into the moving river is swept down the mountain.

Most rivers do not move as fast as they seem to be moving. They travel between 1 to 5 miles, or about 2 to 8 kilometers, an hour. You can pedal a bicycle faster than that.

But even when a river moves slowly, it never stops. As it moves, it wears away the ground under it and on both sides of it. Over the years, a river can wear away miles and miles of land. This wearing away is called *erosion*.

When a river erodes the land, it makes a groove in the ground that is shaped like the letter "V." This V-shape is called a *river valley*.

The river makes the valley deeper. Wind and rain wear away the banks of the river. After thousands of years, the valley is not a V anymore. It looks more like a wide, flat "U." In time, erosion changes a deep, narrow valley into flat land.

Where land is flat, water flows very slowly. But it never stops. There is more water coming down the mountain, pushing at the water ahead of it. The river grows wider and longer as it moves over the land.

When water moves very slowly, it does not carry the bits of rock, sand, and plants from the mountain. These things, called *sediment*, fall to the bottom of the river. If a lot of sediment falls to the same part of the riverbed, a new piece of land will be built up. It will become an island.

Sometimes a river flows into a place where the land is very low. This low land is called a *basin*. When the river water fills the basin, it makes a lake.

Some rivers carry most of the rock and sand and plants all the way to the sea. The sea may be rough at the mouth—or end—of the river. Or the sea may be quiet at the mouth of the river. If it is rough, the sediment will be carried away from the land.

If the sea is quiet, the sediment will stay at the mouth of the river. After a long time, it will build up and become an area of land called a *delta*. The soil of a delta is very rich and makes fine farmland.

Some deltas are small, some are very large. One of the best-known deltas in the world is at the mouth of the Nile River in Egypt.

Egypt is almost all desert. But the Nile Delta has good soil and enough water for farming. That is why most Egyptians live in the Nile Delta.

Every year, before the Aswan Dam was built, the Nile River overflowed its banks. Sand and soil carried by the river were spread over the ground. This ground next to the river is called a *flood plain*. A flood plain has very good soil for plants to grow in.

The yearly flood of the Nile gave Egypt rich soil. But floods can be very bad, too. A long, heavy rain can turn a quiet river into a flood that sweeps away trees, houses, crops, and everything in its path.

There are ways to control the flooding of a river. One way is to build high banks along the sides of the river. These banks, called *levees*, must be higher than the river can rise. There are hundreds of miles of levees along the Mississippi River.

One of the best ways to control a river is to build a *dam*. A dam can be made of stone, of wood, of earth and rocks—anything that will hold back the flow of water.

Beavers are nature's best builders of dams. They build a wall of mud and sticks and stones to stop a river or a stream. This makes a pond for the beavers to live in.

People build huge, strong dams out of concrete. The river water that is held back by a large dam becomes a lake. The lakes made by dams are called *reservoirs*. They reserve, or hold, water. We get our drinking water from reservoirs. A river that is not dammed would carry away this water. Then we would not have enough water in dry seasons.

Some rivers flow at the bottom of a *canyon*. A canyon is a deep, steep river valley. The Grand Canyon, in Arizona, is one of the largest canyons in the world. It is a mile, or 1.6 kilometers, deep and 217 miles, or 347 kilometers, long!

A canyon starts to form when a river erodes dry, rocky land. The water cuts a path that gets deeper and deeper. Millions of years later, the path becomes a canyon.

Rivers run under the ground, too. When they do, they may form *caverns*. A cavern is a hollow place made by water pushing through rock. Some kinds of rock, such as limestone, are very soft. When water runs over this kind of rock, it makes a hole. As time goes by, the hole grows larger and larger until it is a cavern.

Sometimes a river runs over hard rock and then over soft rock. When this happens, the water wears away the soft rock faster than it wears away the hard rock. The water shoots and tumbles over the rocks, forming a *rapid*.

As the river wears away the soft rock, the rapid turns into a *waterfall*. The soft rock has all worn away. Now the water drops straight down from the hard rock at the top.

The Niagara River is part of the border between Canada and the United States. The river itself is small, but it makes Niagara Falls, which is one of nature's marvels. The water spills down, down, down—more than 160 feet, or 48 meters, from top to bottom—in beautiful twin falls.

When water falls a long way, it lands with great force. This force can be used to power the motors that make electricity for homes and factories. Waterfalls, such as Niagara Falls, are used this way.

Rivers have many uses. Before there were cars and planes, people traveled on rivers in boats. Today, most people do not travel by river. But the river is still used to ship products from one place to another. Barges carry coal, steel, grain, and many other things on their flat decks.

People have always settled near rivers. That is because the river gave them water to drink and fish to eat. The river made the land rich for growing plants. It also gave the settlers a way to travel and to trade with other people who used the river.

Our rivers are still important to us. But over the years, some streams and rivers have become dirty, or *polluted*. Many people are working to make our waters clean again.

Rivers are a powerful force on our planet. They build islands, they carve canyons, and they create waterfalls. We use rivers for energy and transportation, too. Swirling and rushing, or gently moving along, rivers are a beautiful and important part of our earth.